THE A-Z

OF

CARAMELS

Commissioning Editor Rose Hewlett
Words by Sophie Berry
Illustrations and Design by Zoë Horn Haywood

ALMONDS

Nuts and caramels go hand in hand, and nuts will give your chewy treats a wonderful crunch. Almonds are a good choice, as the distinctive flavour complements the sweetness of caramels perfectly. Try this classic recipe for chocolate almond caramels.

Chocolate Almond Caramels

Ingredients
1 lb sugar
¼ lb glucose
2 oz butter
½ cup condensed milk
½ cup water
¼ tsp vanilla essence
½ cup almonds, chopped
2 squares chocolate, grated

Method
1. In a heavy-bottomed saucepan heat the sugar, glucose and water to 250°F, or until the mixture forms a firm ball when tested in cold water.

2. Remove the pan from the heat, and add the milk and butter. Stir well.

3. Add the grated chocolate, vanilla essence and chopped almonds, return the pan to the heat and stir well until the the mixture is boiling.

4. Carefully pour the mixture into an oiled baking tin, and mark into squares when cool.

4

BROWN SUGAR

Using brown sugar for your caramels will give your sweets a wonderfully dark, rich colour. This simple recipe for brown sugar caramels also uses molasses, for decadently sweet caramels.

Brown Sugar Caramels

Ingredients
2 ½ tbsp butter
2 cups brown sugar
2 tbsp molasses
½ cup milk
4 squares unsweetened chocolate
1 tsp vanilla essence

Method
1. In a heavy-bottomed saucepan, melt the butter, and then add the sugar, molasses and milk.

2. Bring the mixture to the boil, and add the chocolate. Stir until the chocolate is melted.

3. Heat the mixture until it reaches 250°F, or until the mixture forms a firm ball when tested in cold water.

4. Remove the pan from the heat and add the vanilla essence. Stir well.

5. Carefully pour the mixture into an oiled baking tin, and mark into squares when cool.

CUPS

Lots of recipes will use 'cups' as a measurement. A small coffee cup is perfect for this, and as long as you use the same cup for all measurements, any cup will do.

Below is a handy conversion table:

1 cup	8 fluid ounces	½ pint	237 ml
2 cups	16 fluid ounces	1 pint	474 ml
4 cups	32 fluid ounces	1 quart	946 ml
2 pints	32 fluid ounces	1 quart	0.946 l
4 quarts	128 fluid ounces	1 gallon	3.784 l

DROP TEST

The 'drop test' is when you drop a little mixture into cold water to test the temperature. It's a quick and easy way to see if your caramel is ready to take off the heat. The table below shows what to look out for depending on which final result you want.

Stage	Temperature	Uses
Thread - Forms a thin liquid thread	110°C to 112 °C (230 to 234 °F)	Sugar Syrups
Soft ball - Forms a soft flexible ball that can be flattened.	112°C to 116 °C (234 to 241 °F)	Fudge, pralines, fondant and butter creams
Firm ball - Forms a firm ball that will hold its shape but is still malleable	118°C to 120 °C (244 to 248 °F)	Caramel Candies
Hard ball - Forms thick threads from spoon and creates a hard ball that will hold its shape	121 to 130 °C (250 to 266 °F)	Nougat, marshmallows, gummies, and divinity
Soft crack - Forms firm flexible threads	132°C to 143 °C (270 to 289 °F)	salt water taffy
Hard crack - Forms hard brittle threads that snap easily	146°C to 154 °C (295 to 309 °F)	toffee, brittles, hard candy, and lollipops
Clear liquid - Liquid will begin to change colour. Colour ranges from golden brown to amber	160 °C (320 °F)	caramelised sugar, caramel
Brown liquid - Liquid will begin to change colour. Colour ranges from golden brown to amber	170 °C (338 °F)	caramelised sugar, caramel

EVAPORATED MILK

There are a number of variations of caramels, and the main difference is the use, or absence of cream. Cream caramels are, as their name suggests, creamy and light in colour. Evaporated milk is a common ingredient in cream caramels, and will give your sweets an unmistakably rich flavour. Try this simple and straightforward recipe for evaporated milk caramels.

Caramels with Evaporated Milk

Ingredients
1 ½ cups sugar
1 ½ cups corn syrup
1 ½ cups full-fat milk
1 ½ cups evaporated milk

Method
1. In a large bowl mix the evaporated milk with the full-fat milk.

2. Put 1 ½ cups of the milk mix in a heavy-bottomed saucepan with the sugar and corn syrup and stir over a medium heat until the mixture reaches 240°F, or until the mixture forms a soft ball when tested in cold water.

3. Take the pan off the heat, and add another ¾ cup of the milk mixture you prepared earlier.

4. Return the pan to the hob, and heat until soft-ball stage again.

5. Add the rest of the milk mixture and stir constantly over a low heat.

6. Heat until the mixture reaches 250°F, or until the mixture forms a hard ball when tested in cold water.

7. Remove the pan from the heat, and add the vanilla essence.

8. Carefully pour the mixture into an oiled baking tin, and mark into squares when cool.

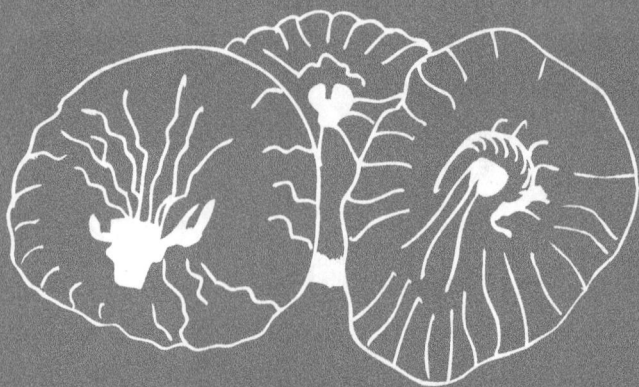

FIG CARAMELS

Fruit works brilliantly alongside the sweet taste of caramels. The addition of fruit not only gives your sweets a more complex flavour, but also adds a pop of colour. This recipe for fruit caramels uses figs, but you can use any dried fruit you like. Raisins, cherries, and cranberries also work really well.

Fruit Caramels

Ingredients
1 lb sugar
4 oz glucose
2 oz butter
½ cup condensed milk
½ cup water
¼ tsp orange essence
4 figs, chopped

Method
1. In a heavy-bottomed saucepan, heat the sugar, glucose and water to 250°F, or until the mixture forms a firm ball when tested in cold water.

2. Remove the pan from the heat, and add the milk and butter. Stir well.

3. Add the figs and essence, return the pan to the heat and stir well until the mixture is boiling.

4. Carefully pour the mixture into an oiled baking tin, and mark into squares when cool.

G

GRANULATED COCONUT

Coconut is a fantastic addition to caramels, as the distinctive flavour complements the sweetness perfectly. Granulated coconut is readily available, and very easy to use in your recipes as all the preparation has been done for you! Try this simple recipe for wonderfully creamy coconut caramels.

Coconut Caramels

Ingredients
1 lb sugar
4 oz glucose
2 oz butter, cubed
2 oz granulated or dessicated coconut, unsweetened
½ cup condensed milk
½ cup water

Method
1. In a heavy-bottomed saucepan, heat the sugar, glucose and water to 250°F, or until the mixture forms a firm ball when tested in cold water.

2. Remove the pan from the heat, and add the milk and butter. Stir well.

3. Add the coconut, return the pan to the heat and stir well until the the mixture is boiling.

4. Carefully pour the mixture into an oiled baking tin, and mark into squares when cool.

HERBS

Caramels are a brilliantly versatile confectionery, and a whole host of flavours can be added to make truly original sweets. You can even add herbs to caramels, giving them a complex taste and lovely aroma. Try this unusual recipe for rosemary caramels, which uses a sprig of the popular garden herb to infuse the mixture with its unmistakable flavour.

Rosemary Caramels

Ingredients

1 sprig fresh rosemary
1 ½ cups double cream
4 oz butter
1 cup light corn syrup
2 cups sugar

1 tsp salt
1 tsp vanilla extract
1 tsp orange zest
½ cup toasted, salted
   pistachios

Method

1. In a heavy-bottomed saucepan, heat the rosemary, cream, and half of the butter over a medium heat. Bring the mixture to a low boil.

2. Remove the pan from the heat and leave the mixture for 45 minutes to infuse the flavours.

3. In a separate smaller pan, heat the sugar and the corn syrup. Stir until the sugar dissolves and the mixture comes to a boil. Heat until the mixture reaches 320°F, or until the mixture remains a clear liquid when tested in cold water.

4. Remove the sugar and syrup pan from the heat. Return to the pan containing the cream, butter and rosemary, and carefully pour the mixture through a strainer into the hot sugar syrup, straining out the rosemary sprig. Be careful not to splash yourself with the hot syrup.

5. Return the pan containing the now-combined ingredients to the heat. Cook the caramel, stirring frequently, until the mixture reaches 250°F, or until the mixture forms a hard ball when tested in cold water.

6. Remove the pan from the heat and stir in the remaining 2 ounces of butter, the salt, the vanilla extract, and the orange zest.

7. Stir in the pistachios. Carefully pour the caramel into a lightly buttered baking tin and mark into squares once cool.

ICE

These caramels are unusual, as they are clear
and colourless. You can fool your party guests by
creating sweet treats which look strikingly like ice
cubes or glass. Making these caramels is a precise
process and requires some impeccable timing.
With this recipe for ice caramels it is imperative
that you don't heat the sugar mixture for too long,
and you remove it from the heat before it starts
taking on a golden hue. If you keep the mixture
cooking too long you will not achieve the unusual
colourless caramel which makes this sweet
so special.

Ice Caramels

Ingredients
½ lb white sugar
½ cup water
½ tsp cream of tartar
½ tsp glucose

Method
1. In a heavy-bottomed saucepan combine the
   sugar and the water and bring to the boil.

2. Add the glucose and cream of tartar and heat the
   mixture until it reaches 310°F, or until the mixture
   forms brittle threads when tested in cold water.

3. Quickly remove the pan from the heat, before the
   mixture starts turning a golden colour, and pour
   into a baking tin lined with baking parchment.

4. Tilt the pan so the mixture covers the entire base.

5. Leave to cool, and break into small pieces
   once hard.

JERSEY CREAM

Using cream or evaporated milk when making caramels will give your sweets a delicious richness. Jersey cream is an extra-thick cream, made from the rich milk Jersey cows produce. Jersey cream caramels are particularly distinctive, as they consist of white caramel, sandwiched between a layer of cream caramel.

Jersey Cream Caramels

Ingredients

For the cream caramel
2 cups white sugar
1 ½ cups corn syrup
2 cups Jersey cream
1 cup butter
1 tsp vanilla essence

For the white caramel
1 cup white sugar
¾ cup corn syrup
1 cup jersey cream
1 cup butter
6 squares white
   chocolate, chopped

Method

1. In a heavy-bottomed saucepan, combine two cups of white sugar, one-and-a-half cups of corn syrup, one cup of butter and one cup of Jersey cream. Bring to a boil, stirring often.

2. Stir in another cup of Jersey cream and heat the mixture to 242° F, or until the mixture forms a soft ball when tested in cold water.

3. Remove the pan from the heat and stir in the vanilla essence.

4. Carefully pour half of the mixture into a lightly buttered baking tin, and return the pan to the stove, over a very low heat.

5. In another heavy-bottomed saucepan, combine one cup of white sugar, three quarters of a cup of corn syrup, one cup of butter and half a cup of Jersey cream. Bring to a boil, stirring often.

6. Drop in the white chocolate and stir until it is melted. Add the remaining Jersey cream, and heat the mixture to 242° F, or until the mixture forms a soft ball when tested in cold water.

7. Carefully pour the white caramel mixture over the first batch of caramel mixture. Leave to cool slightly.

8. Pour the remaining caramel mixture over the white caramel. Cut into squares when cool.

KAHLÚA

Kahlúa is a Mexican coffee-flavoured rum-based liqueur. As an addition to caramels, it is perfect, as the subtle bitterness of the coffee flavour contrasts wonderfully with the sweet taste of caramel. Try this recipe for Kahlúa coffee caramels, which make a fantastic after-dinner treat.

Khalúa Coffee Caramels

Ingredients
2 cups sugar
¼ cups golden syrup
1 cup double cream
¼ cups butter
½ tsp salt
2 tbsp coffee
2 tbsp Khalúa

Method
1. In a heavy-bottomed saucepan, combine all the ingredients.

2. Stir over a low heat until the sugar has dissolved.

3. Heat the mixture until it reaches 250°F, or until the mixture forms a firm ball when tested in cold water.

4. Carefully pour the mixture into a lightly buttered baking tin.

5. Mark into squares when cool.

LAYERS

Once you have a little experience making caramels, you can really get creative and try making layered sweets, similar to the Jersey caramels we mentioned earlier in this book. This recipe for layered peanut caramels has a smooth, nutty layer atop the classic vanilla-based caramel. You could try dipping your finished caramels in melted chocolate, for a decorative touch.

Layered Peanut Caramels

Ingredients

Caramel layer
1 lb sugar
4 oz glucose
2 oz butter
½ cup evaporated milk
½ cup water
¼ tsp vanilla essence

Peanut layer
1 cup smooth peanut
   butter
1 cup evaporated milk
½ cup peanuts,
   chopped

Method

1. In a heavy-bottomed saucepan, heat the glucose and water to 250°F, or until the mixture forms a firm ball when tested in cold water.

2. Remove the pan from the heat, and add half a cup of evaporated milk and butter. Stir well.

3. Add the vanilla essence, return the pan to the heat and stir well until the the mixture is boiling.

4. Carefully pour the mixture into a baking tin, lined with baking parchment.

5. Set aside to cool slightly. You want the caramel to be firm, but not hard.

6. In another heavy-bottomed saucepan, combine the the peanut butter, one cup of evaporated milk and the peanuts and stir over a low heat.

7. When the ingredients are combined, and the mixture is smooth, take the pan off the heat and carefully pour over the semi-cooled caramel.

8. Leave the mixture to set in the fridge, and mark into squares before completely cooled.

MAPLE

Maple sugar is made from the sap of sugar-maple trees and is a traditional sweetener in America and Canada. Maple sugar is almost twice as sweet as regular cane sugar, making it a fantastic addition to many sweet recipes. This recipe for maple caramels uses a mixture of sugars, which will subtly flavour your caramels with the unmistakable taste of maple.

M

Maple Caramels

Ingredients
cup maple sugar
cup white sugar
½ cup corn syrup
2 cups single cream

Method
1. In a heavy-bottomed saucepan, heat the sugar, corn syrup, and half a cup of the cream over a low heat. Stir until the sugar has dissolved.

2. Bring the mixture to the boil, and heat until to 240°F, or until the mixture forms a soft ball when tested in cold water.

3. Add another half cup of cream, stirring constantly.

4. Bring the mixture back to the boil, and when the mixture again reaches 240°F, or forms a soft ball when tested in cold water, add the remaining cream.

5. Heat the mixture to 250°F, or until the mixture forms a firm ball when tested in cold water.

6. Carefully pour the mixture into an oiled baking tin, and mark into squares when cool.

N

NUTS

Nuts are a wonderful addition to your caramels. When using nuts in your recipe, make sure they are unsalted, and chopped coarsely. Chopping the nuts too finely will make the sweets take on an almost gritty texture. You want them to retain some of their shape, but not overpower the sweets. A very quick blitz in a food processor is a quick and easy way to prepare your nut meats.

Walnut Caramels

Ingredients
1 lb sugar
½ cup shelled walnuts, chopped
4 oz glucose
2 oz butter, cubed
¼ tsp saffron food colouring
½ cup condensed milk
½ cup water

Method
1. In a heavy-bottomed saucepan, heat the sugar, glucose and water to 250°F, or until the mixture forms a firm ball when tested in cold water.

2. Remove the pan from the heat, and add the milk and butter. Stir well.

3. Add the walnuts and essence, return the pan to the heat and stir well until the the mixture is boiling.

4. Carefully pour the mixture into an oiled baking tin, and mark into squares when cool.

OPERA CARAMELS

The term 'opera caramels' dates back to the 1920s, when sugar-based treats such as caramels were hugely popular. Opera caramels would have been carefully prepared at home and taken out to be enjoyed by adults while at the opera. Homemade caramels were a popular treat for children as well. Many youngsters looked forward to their Saturday trip to the pictures, armed with a penny to buy a ticket and a little bag of sweets.

Opera Caramels

Ingredients
1 cup light brown sugar
1 cup raisins
4 cups single cream

Method
1. In a heavy-bottomed saucepan, heat the sugar and cream over a medium heat.

2. Heat the mixture until it is 240°F, or until the mixture forms a soft ball when tested in cold water.

3. Carefully pour the mixture into a lightly buttered baking tin, and sprinkle the raisins over.

4. Using a spatula or wooden spoon, press down on the surface of the mixture so the raisins mix well with the caramel.

P

PEPPERMINT

The fresh flavour of peppermint is a fantastic addition to caramels, and will give your sweet treats a real kick. Adding peppermint to your caramels also makes the sweets a perfect after-dinner offering.

Peppermint Caramels

Ingredients
1 lb sugar
4 oz glucose
2 oz butter
½ cup condensed milk
½ cup water
¼ tsp peppermint oil

Method
1. In a heavy-bottomed saucepan, heat the sugar, glucose and water to 250°F, or until the mixture forms a firm ball when tested in cold water.

2. Remove the pan from the heat, and add the milk and butter. Stir well.

3. Add the peppermint oil, return the pan to the heat and stir well until the the mixture is boiling.

4. Carefully pour the mixture into an oiled baking tin, and mark into squares when cool.

LIQUEUR

There are a number of different types of caramels. Caramel is a sauce, rather than a sweet and is a brilliant recipe to master as it can be used to add flavour to a whole host of puddings. Try this incredibly simple recipe for liqueur caramel sauce, which can transform a simple serving of vanilla ice cream into an indulgent dessert. You can use any liqueur you like, but Khalúa, Grand Marnier or Bailey's work especially well.

<u>Liqueur Caramel Sauce</u>

<u>Ingredients</u>
2 cups light brown sugar
1 cup butter
1 cup double cream
1 tbsp liqueur

<u>Method</u>
1. In a heavy-bottomed saucepan, combine the sugar and butter and heat gently.

2. When the sugar has dissolved, take the pan off the heat, and slowly add the cream.

3. Whisk the mixture, whilst slowly adding the liqueur.

4. Return the pan to the hob, over a very low heat. Heat the mixture gently for two minutes, stirring all the time.

5. Remove the pan from the heat, and serve your sauce as soon as possible.

R

RASPBERRIES

Fruity caramels are a real treat, and adding fruit to your sweets will give them a lovely pop of colour. This recipe for raspberry caramels rather ingeniously uses jam, and a little red food colouring to make for a distinctive sweet. Why not get creative, and try substituting raspberry jam for another fruit conserve?

<u>Raspberry Caramels</u>

<u>Ingredients</u>
1 lb sugar
4 oz glucose.
2 oz butter, cubed
¼ tsp red food colouring
4 oz raspberry jam
½ cup condensed milk
½ cup water

<u>Method</u>
1. In a heavy-bottomed saucepan, heat the sugar, glucose and water to 250°F, or until the mixture forms a firm ball when tested in cold water.

2. Remove the pan from the heat, and add the milk, butter and jam. Stir well,

3. Add the colouring, return the pan to the heat and stir well until the the mixture is boiling.

4. Carefully pour the mixture into an oiled baking tin, and mark into squares when cool.

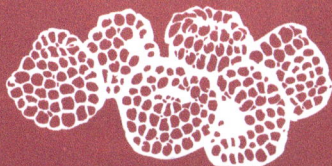

SALTED CARAMELS

Salt may not sound like an obvious addition to a recipe for caramels, but the bold contrast in flavours actually works rather well. Salt complements the sweetness of caramels, giving your sweets a complex, refined flavour and making them rather moreish! A coarse, natural sea salt is the best kind to use, and hidden in the middle of your sweets will give them a brilliantly crunchy texture.

Salted Caramels

Ingredients
1 lb sugar
4 oz glucose
2 oz butter
½ cup condensed milk
½ cup water
¼ tsp vanilla essence
1 tbsp coarse sea salt

Method
1. In a heavy-bottomed saucepan, heat the sugar, glucose and water to 250°F, or until the mixture forms a firm ball when tested in cold water.

2. Remove the pan from the heat, and add the milk and butter. Stir well.

3. Add the essence, return the pan to the heat and stir well until the the mixture is boiling.

4. Carefully pour half of the mixture into an oiled baking tin.

5. Sprinkle the top of your caramel mixture with the sea salt.

6. Pour the remaining mixture over the top of the salt and leave to cool.

7. Mark into squares before it sets completely.

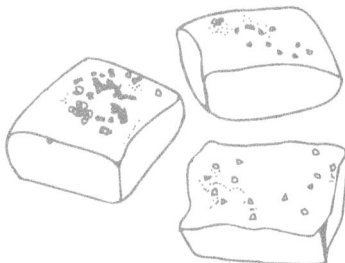

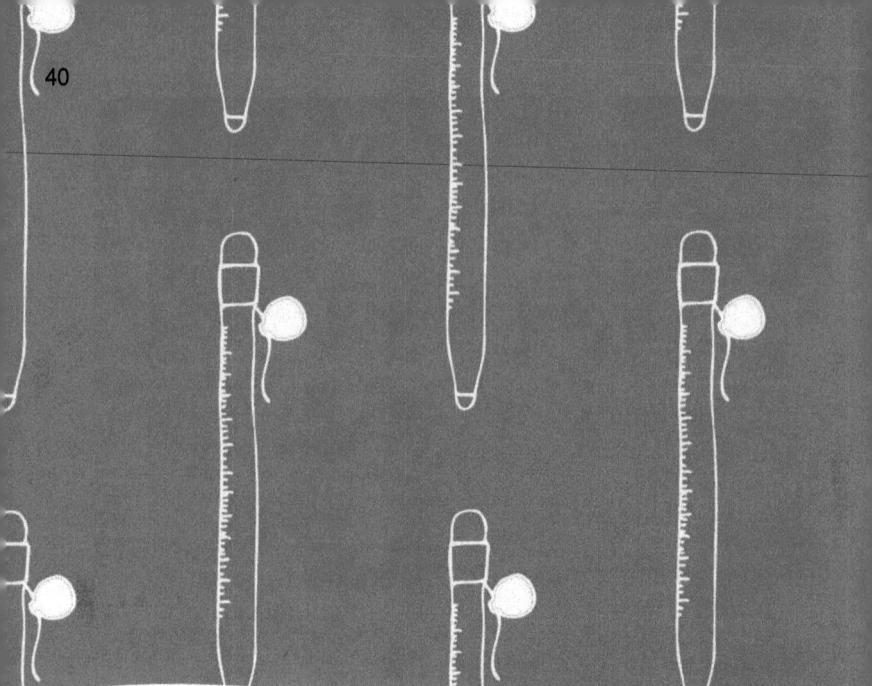

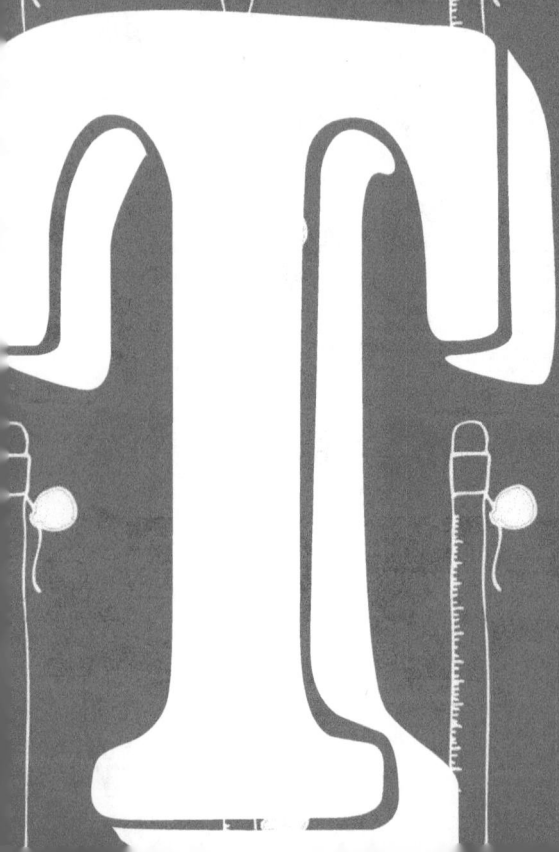

THERMOMETER

A thermometer is the best way to test the temperature of your caramel mixture. Although you can test caramel by dropping a little mixture into cold water, a thermometer is far more accurate especially as the temperature of cooking sugar can soar extremely quickly.

Be careful not to undercook or overcook your caramels. Temperature is very important in sweet making, just a few degrees either way can result in a completely different final product. If your mixture is heated to less than 240°F you should return the pan to the heat, and carefully take the temperature of your mixture a little higher until it reaches 250°F. Under cooking your caramel mixture may result in fudge, and if leave the mixture too long, it will become too hot and you may result in a much harder sweet such as toffee.

It is important to break in a new thermometer. Put it into a pan of cold water, bring the pan to the boil, and leave it there until the water has cooled. After using your thermometer to test the temperature of cooking sugar mixture, plunge it into warm water and wipe it straight away.

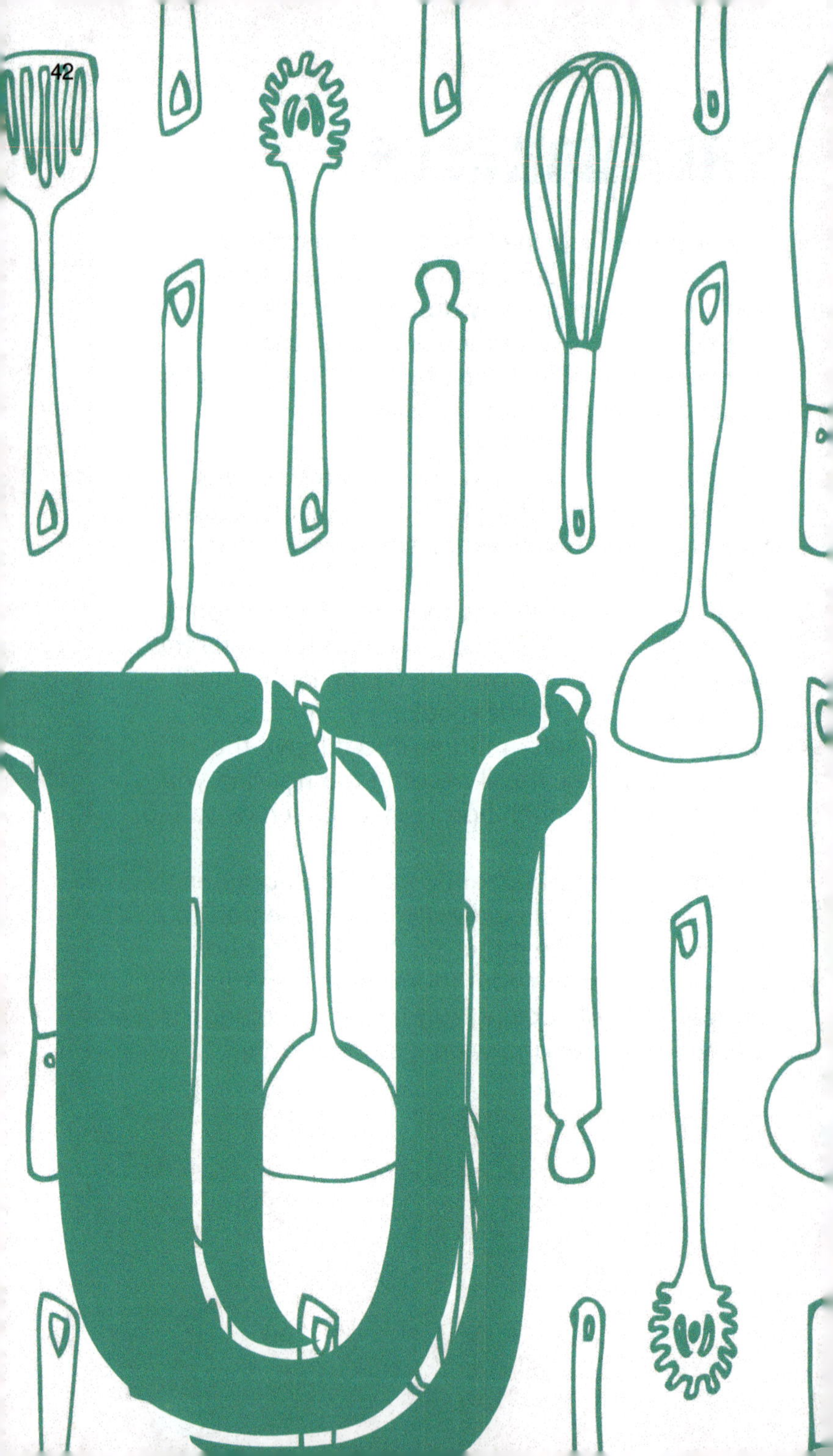
U

UTENSILS

Good utensils are essential when you are making caramels. A wooden spoon or spatula is essential for stirring the hot mixture as it cooks, as plastic utensils won't withstand the high temperature of the boiling sugar. A sharp knife will also be useful when you come to cutting your caramels into small pieces.

When making caramels, you will need a good baking tin. A large, shallow tin is best, so you can spread your caramel out into a fairly thin layer. A small, deep tin will mean your mixture will take longer to cool, and your sweets may be too chunky! Lining your tins with baking paper as well as lightly greasing them with butter or vegetable oil will stop the mixture sticking to the sides.

You will also need to make sure you have the basics when it comes to equipment. A heavy-bottomed saucepan is essential, and you'll need another, smaller saucepan for some of the recipes in this book.

VANILLA

The subtle sweetness of vanilla is a perfect flavour to add to your caramels. Indeed, vanilla essence is the base flavour of many a caramels recipe, and helps to complement the sweetness of the confectionery. You can experiment with using other flavours and essences in when making your sweets, but vanilla is the perfect starting point for a caramel-making novice.

Vanilla Caramels

Ingredients
1 lb sugar
4 oz glucose
2 oz butter
½ cup condensed milk
½ cup water
¼ tsp vanilla essence

Method
1. In a heavy-bottomed saucepan, heat the sugar, glucose and water to 250°F, or until the mixture forms a firm ball when tested in cold water.

2. Remove the pan from the heat, and add the milk and butter. Stir well.

3. Add the vanilla essence, return the pan to the heat and stir well until the the mixture is boiling.

4. Carefully pour the mixture into an oiled baking tin, and mark into squares when cool.

WARTIME

During the second world war food supplies in the UK dwindled due to trade ships being intercepted. Sugar was one of the first foodstuffs to be rationed, which it was on the 8th January, 1940. This meant that sweets became a rare treat in wartime Britain, and some ingenious mothers took to creating sweet substitutes in their kitchens, using fruit and vegetables for their natural sugars.

Surprisingly, potato is a fantastic addition to caramels, as the starch in the ground vegetable will give your sweets a firm texture, without having an overpowering taste. If you don't have a potato ricer, you can use a coarse cheese grater to prepare your spuds, or try pushing the cooked potato through a metal sieve or colander.

Potato Caramels

Ingredients
½ lb sugar
½ cup milk
½ cup boiled, riced potato
1 tbsp butter
¼ tsp salt

Method
1. In a heavy-bottomed saucepan, heat all of the ingredients except the milk.

2. Boil the mixture until it thickens, and add half a cup of milk.

3. Bring the mixture to the boil again, and when it thickens add another half cup of milk.

4. Heat the mixture again until it reaches 250°F, or until the mixture forms a firm ball when tested in cold water.

5. Carefully pour the mixture into an oiled baking pan, and mark into squares when cool.

XMAS

Christmas is a perfect time to get a batch of caramels cooking. You can carefully wrap and package your homemade caramels, making them a perfect gift for adults and children alike. This recipe for Christmas caramels uses dried cranberries and angelica to give your sweets a fantastically festive pop of colour, but you can use any jewel-coloured dried fruits you like.

Christmas Caramels

Ingredients
1 lb sugar
4 oz glucose
2 oz butter
½ cup condensed milk
½ cup water
¼ tsp cinnamon essence
1 tbsp dried cranberries, chopped
1 tbsp angelica, chopped

Method
1. In a heavy-bottomed saucepan, heat the sugar, glucose and water to 250°F, or until the mixture forms a firm ball when tested in cold water.

2. Remove the pan from the heat, and add the milk and butter. Stir well.

3. Add the cinnamon syrup, return the pan to the heat and stir well until the the mixture is boiling.

4. Remove from the heat, and add the cranberries and angelica. Stir well.

5. Carefully pour the mixture into an oiled baking tin, and mark into squares when cool.

YANKEE

Marshmallows are a fun addition to your caramels, and will give your sweets a slightly light and fluffy texture. This recipe uses large marshmallows, cut into quarters, but you can use multi-coloured mini marshmallows for a sweet treat that children will love.

Marshmallow Caramels

Ingredients
1 lb sugar
4 oz glucose
2 oz butter
½ cup condensed milk
½ cup water
¼ tsp cinnamon syrup
8 large marshmallows, chopped into quarters

Method
1. In a heavy-bottomed saucepan, heat the sugar, glucose and water to 250°F, or until the mixture forms a firm ball when tested in cold water.

2. Remove the pan from the heat, and add the milk and butter. Stir well.

3. Add the essence, return the pan to the heat and stir well until the the mixture is boiling.

4. Remove from the heat, and add the marshmallows. Stir well.

5. Carefully pour the mixture into an oiled baking tin, and mark into squares when cool.

ZEST

The zest of a citrus fruit is a fabulous addition to your homemade caramels, and adds a hint of colour as well as a great, zingy taste to your sweets. You can use the zest of any fruit you wish, but a mixture of zest can create a brilliantly bright batch of caramels.

Zesty Caramels

Ingredients
1 lb sugar
4 oz glucose
2 oz butter
½ cup condensed milk
½ cup water
¼ tsp lemon essence
1 tbsp citrus zest

Method
1. In a heavy-bottomed saucepan, heat the sugar, glucose and water to 250ºF, or until the mixture forms a firm ball when tested in cold water.

2. Remove the pan from the heat, and add the milk and butter. Stir well.

3. Add the vanilla essence, return the pan to the heat and stir well until the the mixture is boiling.

4. Carefully pour the mixture into an oiled baking tin, and sprinkle over the citrus zest.

5. Mark into squares when cool

TOP TEN TIP:

1. Buy a thermometer – It will make your caramel-making a lot simpler, and much more accurate.

2. Make sure you 'break in' a new thermometer. Put the thermometer into a pan of cold water, bring the pan to the boil, and leave it there until the water has cooled.

3. After using your thermometer to test the temperature, plunge it into warm water and wipe it straight away.

4. Have all your ingredients measured and ready before you begin. Making caramels needs much precision, and having everything ready will ensure nothing is overcooked.

5. Follow the recipe exactly. Until you have a lot of experience making caramels, it is best to follow recipes exactly. When you become more confident, you can experiment with your own variations.

AND TRICKS

6. Make sure you remember to grease your baking tin well with vegetable oil or butter before pouring the mixture in to cool.

7. If you are worried about the mixture sticking to the pan, line it with baking paper and grease the baking paper, too.

8. Once you have poured the mixture out of the pan, immediately fill the pan with hot water and return it to the heat for a few minutes. This will stop your mixture setting onto the pan and will make it a lot easier to clean.

9. Wrapping your caramels individually in either cellophane or baking paper will stop them sticking together while they are being stored.

10. It is best to store your caramels somewhere cool.

Two Magpies

Copyright © 2013 Two Magpies Publishing
An imprint of Read Publishing Ltd
Home Farm, 44 Evesham Road, Cookhill, Alcester,
Warwickshire, B49 5LJ

Commissioning Editor Rose Hewlett
Words by Sophie Berry
Design and Illustrations by Zoë Horn Haywood

British Library Cataloguing-in-Publication Data A
catalogue record for this book is available from the
British Library.

www.ingramcontent.com/pod-product-compliance
Lightning Source LLC
Chambersburg PA
CBHW051434090426
42737CB00014B/2968